JOHN RILEY

THE MASTER DRUMMER

EXPANDED EDITION

HOW TO PRACTICE, PLAY AND THINK LIKE A PRO

By John Riley

Executive producer: Rob Wallis

Book layout: Terry Branam

Music transcriptions and engraving: Terry Branam

Updated cover design: Terry Branam

Edited by Joe Bergamini

Videographer: Tony Scimeca

Cover photos:

Front top: Nick Meyer

Front bottom: Jules Follett

Back cover: Nick Meyer

VIDEO & AUDIO DOWNLOAD

To download video & audio:

Go To: halleonard.com/mylibrary

Enter Code: 8523-8258-0363-8780

CONTENTS ▶

INTRODUCTION

I fell in love with music and the drums a long time ago and have been an observer, student and fan of great drummers for over 40 years. In that time I've come to realize that all the great players have seamlessly assimilated four main components of music-making, and they play with a spirit that unifies and inspires their bandmates. This book will dig into each of these critical components. I'll show you exercises and strategies that have been beneficial to me and I'm certain will help you achieve your musical goals.

The drum set is a relatively young instrument—it's only about 100 years old—and up until the 1960s, everyone that played the drum set was a jazz drummer. So the jazz drumming language is the foundation for most of what's played today and, as such, the basis for this book. If you already own my books *The Art of Bop Drumming*, *Beyond Bop Drumming* and *The Jazz Drummer's Workshop*, this book will expand on that material and shed light on areas the books don't address. If you don't own my books, they are chock full of useful information which will be a great supplement to the material presented here.

The drums are a very powerful instrument, but we're primarily an accompanying instrument—our job is to help make the band sound as good as possible. Since a band really IS only as good as its drummer, what does it take to become a great player, a master musician of the drum set?

It should go without saying that one must have a love of music and of playing the drums and a curiosity about how the music and drumming have evolved. As I've said, I've come to realize that all great players share four fundamental qualities: They all have excellent technique, a strong groove, fluid creativity and superior musicianship. The development of each of these characteristics is essential because they work together when playing at the highest level. Whether you dream of playing with Miles or Meshuggah, you've got to have good time and an understanding of songs in order to be a contender, so the development of your groove and musicianship must not be overlooked in the pursuit of the more tantalizing skills.

Practicing should focus primarily on groove and musicianship, but this instrument is a little too complicated to be successful at without a certain level of technical control. Technique and creativity are the building blocks which lead to a solid groove and contribute to good musicianship. Improved technique improves your groove and makes it possible to execute your musical decisions. Superior technique doesn't necessarily lead to great musicality, but most of the innovators, on all instruments, are able to hear things their peers can't and are able to execute their innovations because their technique is superior.

CHAPTER 1: Technique ▶

Hand Technique

So what do I mean by technique? In the broadest sense, having good technique means having control of each of your limbs so that you can organize them to best support the music you are playing, but let's start with some the fundamentals of hand technique.

There are two different philosophies on how to move the sticks. The first I'll call the "firm grip" and it's basic premise is to control the movement of the stick at all times. In the firm grip the fingers are wrapped around the stick throughout the entire range of motion. Muscles are engaged to lower the stick towards the drum and to lift the stick back to the starting point. The result is great precision and a dry, staccato sound.

The second approach I call the "loose grip." It seeks to capitalize on the fact that, when held loosely, the stick wants to rebound. My fingers engage the stick with just enough contact to avoid losing it. I throw the stick towards the drum and let it fly into the surface. After it strikes the surface, the ensuing momentum propels it back to the starting point. The result is a more legato sound and, with ample practice, equal control and better endurance than with the firm grip.

You may find it helpful to cultivate the feeling of the rebounding the stick, if you experiment with throwing the stick while loosely holding it between your index and middle fingers. Once you can feel that free-flowing motion, return the stick to the normal position and cultivate that same sensation.

For softer, faster playing I rotate my hand from the palm-down German grip to the thumb-up French grip and initiate each stroke with my middle finger. All my fingers contribute, but the middle finger is the prime driver of the stick.

If you play matched grip, use your right hand as a model for your left. I play traditional grip and find it helpful to cultivate the sensation of the rebounding stick by first holding the left stick with my thumb and simply rotating my wrist.

Kengo Photos

Vanguard Jazz Orchestra, Japan, 2012

Once that motion feels relaxed, I reposition the stick, cradling it — not clamping down on it — in the webbing of my left hand and gently curve my index finger over the stick. With the traditional grip, the index finger is the main point of contact and the initiator of both wrist strokes and finger strokes. The other fingers should simply find a natural relaxed position.

The balance of your stick has a big impact on just how much rebound you get. Check out the relationship between the speed of each downstroke and each rebounding upstroke. To me it looks and feels as if the stick is actually rebounding up even faster than it's going down. Check out that same relationship when I flip my stick over and play with the heavier butt end. In this position the stick definitely feels slower. That means in order to play fast I'll need to use my muscles more to compensate for the stick's slower upward momentum. I imagine that you, like me, prefer to let the stick do as much of the work as possible, so I suggest you select a stick that feels as lively as possible. In general, sticks that feel top-heavy are more sluggish.

We've discussed a little bit about wrist and finger strokes and hand positions. Where does volume come from? Volume comes from height. When a coin is dropped from two inches, we get less volume than when it's dropped from twelve inches, and it's the same with a stick. If I need more volume I will add more height by simply raising my arm, or I will add the weight of my forearm to the movement.

Hopefully by now you have a sense of just how gently to hold the sticks. As you start to work on these ideas you will most likely feel that you will be giving up too much control if you hold your sticks as loosely as I hold mine. If this is the case, I suggest you put a little stick wax on your sticks. I find that when I first start playing each day, or if I'm in an extremely air-conditioned room, my sticks feel slippery. After a few minutes of playing, a little perspiration builds up and the sticks feel much more secure. I find the application of a little stick wax makes the sticks feel great right away.

Most of my playing, maybe 80%, is with the wrists and in a more-or-less German position on the snare drum. I rotate my right hand into a French, or what some people refer to as the ¾ American grip, to play the ride cymbal so that I can incorporate my fingers. To play the ride cymbal, I use the combination of a wrist throw on beats 2 and 4, and then I collect the stick with my fingers to play the skip note and beats 1 and 3. The motion starts on beat 2.

Even if you are relaxed, any kind of repetitive movement, like a long series of wrist strokes or a long series of finger strokes, will lead to fatigue. Because I am distributing the workload between a wrist throw and the finger action when playing the ride cymbal, I can get a really good sound and play quite fast and relaxed for long periods of time.

The Moeller Stroke

Another movement which distributes the workload is the Moeller stroke. In the Moeller stroke the arm or forearm employs a whipping motion which causes the wrist to accelerate and snap towards the drum. This whipping stroke generates enough energy to create multiple secondary bounces. If one's wrist and fingers are supple enough to accept these "free" notes, the Moeller stroke can be a great addition to your playing.

One of the difficulties in mastering the Moeller stroke is that, in order to get it, you've got to really give up a lot of your control of the stick. One effective way to overcome this problem is to do exercises which give your brain something else to worry about while you make the Moeller stroke. The idea is that if your brain is preoccupied with another activity, the hand playing the Moeller stroke will have to relax and find its own natural equilibrium.

Since the Moeller stroke is best mastered as a three-note sequence, let's imagine we are playing eighth notes in 3/4 and accenting every third eighth note, like this: (sing **1**+2+**3**+)

Now, with your opposite hand, play the three quarter notes in each bar while maintaining the Moeller sequence. At first there will be a lot of friction between your limbs, but eventually the hand playing Moeller will find its own sense of balance and order. Don't force the synchronization of your hands; let them work it out together.

Once this is flowing, try varying the pattern in your opposite hand. Now make the Moeller sequence in triplets and vary your opposite hand.

The Moeller stroke is great, but it doesn't work in every musical situation simply because the stroke is powered by an accented first note. Years ago Joe Morello showed me how he could diminish that accent by minimizing and randomizing the whipping motion in his left hand. This mini-Moeller stroke almost becomes a shimmying movement, where the left index finger simply rides on top of the stick.

We've been talking about hand technique, which is a large subject. If you'd like to delve further into this I recommend checking out: Joe Morello's *A Natural Approach to Technique* and Jojo Mayer's *Secret Weapons for the Modern Drummer*.

Foot Technique

Now I'd like to discuss a little bit about foot technique. I'm using basically the same approach with the bass drum as I use with my hands. On the bass drum pedal I am playing heel down and I launch the beater towards the bass drum head, let it fly into the head and bounce off. With a bass drum tuned like this, with some resonance, this approach generates the best sound. I don't press the beater into the head, because that chokes the sound of the drum and reduces my speed and flexibility. Most of my playing is flat-footed.

The way I generate power on the bass drum pedal is the same as the way I do it with the sticks, I use height, or in this case I make my pedal strokes longer. At a loud volume the beater is almost starting from the top of my shoe. So, just like with the hands, I use smaller strokes to play softly and larger strokes to play louder. Regardless of the volume, I strive to get a good sound and to stay relaxed.

For years I had difficulty listening to the old-timers like Gene Krupa, Buddy Rich and even Max Roach because they played the bass drum so loudly when they played four on the floor. I asked Jim Chapin about this, and his answer was really enlightening. Jim told me that in those days the bandleaders didn't trust the projection of their bass players, so band leaders sought out drummers with a strong foot to compensate. Drummers had to play the bass drum strongly or they wouldn't get hired.

Playing the hi-hat is a little different, because what we are generally going for is a staccato sound, so we have to use either pressure or weight to get a clean "chick." There are three different approaches to achieving a good chick. The technique many jazz drummers use we call the heel-toe technique, so if you are playing 2 and 4 on the hi-hat, your heel will tap beats 1 and 3 while your toe will play beats 2 and 4. When you synchronize that with your bass drum, your left heel should land exactly with the bass drum on beats 1 and 3.

Another way to play the hi-hat is with a rocking motion. My heel is lifted off the pedal but I maintain some weight on the cymbals. I rock my heel up and down and gently release the weight off of the cymbals just before beats 2 and 4 so that the cymbals

Dario Guerini

Carnegie Hall Jazz Band, Italy, 1995

open. The weight is then brought back in on beats 2 and 4 to create a good chick. When synchronized with the bass drum, it looks like this: ▶

This is an excellent technique for playing up tempos, because the rocking movement of the entire leg helps us stay relaxed and the added weight helps us get a solid chick.

For softer playing I don't need as much weight on the pedal so I play the hi-hat flat-footed. The movement looks like this: ▶

I like to set up my hi-hat with the top cymbal fairly loose in the clutch and with the cymbals about two inches apart. This loose top cymbal generates a warm, open sound when playing time on the hi-hat, when splashing the hi-hat, and when using the hi-hat as a crash sound.

Coordination

PLAY-ALONGS

So we've discussed a little bit about hand technique, a little bit about foot technique; the next technical component is coordination. The objective is to gain control of your limbs so that you can play either hand or either foot at any time in the service of the music—that's the ultimate goal. So I'd like to show you a series of exercises with that in mind; first with the cymbal playing time and the feet playing time while the left hand plays a moving part, then we'll take it from there.

Since we're working towards playing music, these exercises should be practiced as four-measure phrases, and you should strive to be able to hear a four-bar structure. I've asked the great bass player Jay Anderson to play some bass lines at a variety of tempos for you to practice with, and I'll play along with them too. For now we'll focus on one simple harmonic structure which we call the 1-6-2-5 turnaround, or C A D G, because this harmonic cycle is part of many songs. We're going to use this cycle in many ways to develop coordination and later to work on groove.

So that's a collection of basic, classic jazz comping phrases. You want to get comfortable with them and not let your ride cymbal distort as you play them. The next thing to do is to play the exact same sequence with the bass drum.

It's necessary to develop the ability to play running lines of eighth notes between your snare drum and bass drum against the cymbal and hi-hat pattern, so now I'm going to demonstrate a series of combinations of 1 note with the hand, 1 note with the foot, 2 notes with the hand, 2 notes with the foot and 3 notes with the hand, 1 note with the foot.

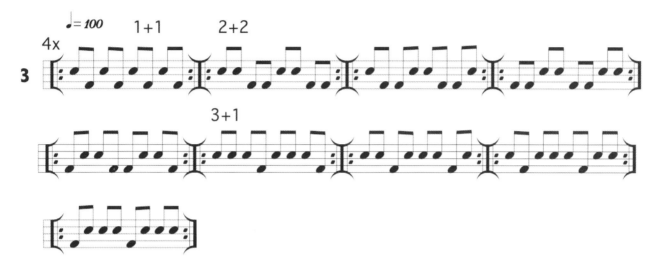

Notice that when I play these running lines of eighth notes, the spacing of my snare drum and bass drum has the same kind of triplet swing feel as the way I play the cymbal pattern.

Here's one more phrase to check out: 2 notes with the hand and 1 note with the foot.

Once you are comfortable with this collection of 1+1, 2+1, 2+2, and 3+1, the next step is to improvise with these ideas. While thinking in four-bar phrases, add rests inside the combinations and try to create a flowing melodic line between your snare drum and bass drum, like this:

CHAPTER 1 (continued)

Headroom ▶

When you see a great player play, there's an ease to what they are doing. The ideas they are playing may be incredibly complicated, but there's a flow to the execution that comes from a familiarity with and mastery of the material they are playing.

There's a concept called "headroom," which comes from the automotive world. Headroom refers to excess capacity: If you have a car that is capable of a maximum speed of 60 miles an hour, when you're going 60 miles an hour, that car is doing everything it is capable of, there is no excess capacity. A car capable of going 200 miles an hour just breezes along at 60 because it has all that headroom from 61-200 miles an hour in reserve. The same concept applies in drumming; you want to have more capabilities than are required to perform your role in a band, so that that role is almost physically effortless and your brainpower can be dedicated to focusing on supporting the other musicians. With that in mind, I'd like to play that same series of 1+1, 2+2 and 3+1 double-time so we can see what the potential is there.

You can up the ante even further, and increase your headroom, if you play the same ideas at a triplet rate in double-time, like this:

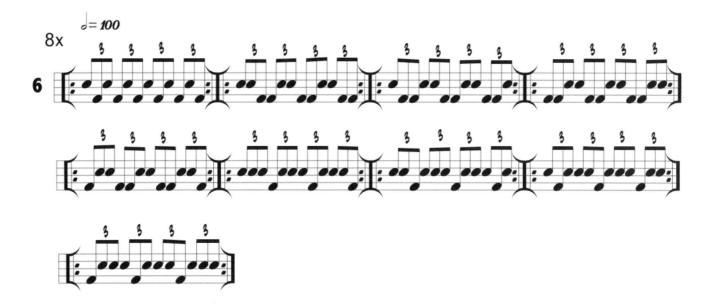

This isn't music, it's the process of getting control of your limbs. Let's take the idea of incorporating these phrases in a musical context like we have to do on the job, like we have to do with a band. I'm going to play a drum version of the song "Mary had a Little Lamb." I'm using that melody as a director for when I play the snare drum and when I play the bass drum. I'll start out with a very simple version, gradually embellish it, and show you how all the coordination phrases can be incorporated to fortify a melody.

"MARY"

Thus far we've been dealing with symmetrical phrases: combinations of 1+1, 2+2, etc. To enhance your headroom, and the capacity to play anything you can hear, it's also helpful to play odd-grouped phrases like 5-note or 7-note ideas. A 5-note phrase could be 4 notes with the hand, 1 note with the foot, or 3+2 or 2,1,1,1. Let me play these combinations for you.

You can do the same kind of thing with groups of 7 notes: 6+1, 5+2, 4+3 etc.

Here's a collection of 5- and 7-note phrases, each played for eight measures.

6+1

5+2

4+3

2+2+2+1

To increase your orchestration possibilities, go through all of these sequences with the hi-hat replacing the bass drum. Some of the double-and triple-note things are not going to be so practical when played with the hi-hat, but getting the brain to send the signals to the left foot early enough to execute them will be good training.

Another way to use these ideas is to play the hands in unison while inserting the bass drum or hi-hat in-between. These combinations would look like this:

Conclusion—The Gift

Listening to and studying the masters is what informs me and inspires me to explore all the different possibilities of the drum set. Occasionally I'll hear someone say that they will never be able to play as well as their idols because they are not "gifted" like their idols are. To that I respond: "What's the gift that those people have and you don't?" Sure some people are born with superior reflexes

Nick Meyer

Range Recording, Ardmore, PA, 2009

or perfect pitch, but those things are meaningless if not cultivated. I think the gift our idols possess is really more a matter of disposition than physical attributes. The gifted are the lucky few who have found something that they are passionate about. So passionate, in fact, that they are compelled to investigate it whether anyone else is interested or not. Their temperament allows them to spend countless hours and years refining their craft by practicing the things they can't do simply because that process is the thing they find most enjoyable in life. That's the gift.

In the Woodshed

Refer to page 60 for a complete transcription and breakdown.

CHAPTER 2: Groove ▶

Micro and Macro Timing

So what is groove? Obviously there is a metronomic component, but there is also an emotional or psychological component too. On the metronomic side of things, we have the micro dimension—that's the fine placement of the partials of each beat. That's strengthened by doing the coordination exercises we were just dealing with, because they were designed to reduce the friction between your limbs so that you can synchronize your ideas in a flowing way. The macro dimension deals with the bigger picture: the consistent overall pulse and tempo from the beginning of a song to the end of the song.

The pulse or tempo of a song is established by the count-off. If the drummer is not the person giving the count-off, we must be very alert to the person that is counting the song off. We've all had the experience of playing a song and getting towards the end only to realize that the tempo is considerably faster or slower than when we started. At that point there is nothing you can do to rectify the situation. What I find really helps me maintain a steady pulse is to use the melody, and specifically the feeling of the flow of the melody, as a kind of click track. As the melody is being

Niels Christiensen

played for the first time, I let the feeling of the flow of the melody imprint on me—I memorize the sound and feeling of that melody. Then, as the song progresses, I am continually singing the melody to myself and making sure that it flows just like it did the first time through. If it starts to a little feel strange to me along the way, I can gradually finesse it back to the original tempo without it becoming a big event. Singing the melody also has the added benefits of making it impossible to lose your place in the song and it gives you a context and good content for your comping ideas. All the great players are aware of the melody as they are playing.

John Scofield, England, 1990

So we've spoken about the micro and the macro aspects of groove. The emotional element involves both the players and the listeners. In order for the pulse of an ensemble to gel, each individual musician must suppress their natural instinct to want to grab the spotlight. Playing strong, but for the good of the whole, is the key.

From the listener's prospective, the groove is the thing that draws most to the music in the first place. You've got a pulse, and once the listener can feel the pulse and begin to anticipate where the next "one" is, they start to relax. When a band is really grooving, the pulse becomes hypnotic and captivates the listener to the point where their daily concerns evaporate. Grooving music, like a great Spielberg movie, provides a much-needed escape from reality, and that's the real reason people go to concerts and buy CDs.

PLAY-ALONGS

Groove Exercise #1

Now that we've discussed the various components of groove, I'd like to show you a couple exercises to further strengthen your sense of pulse. The first one involves using some simple comping phrases, like those at the beginning of this book, and playing them in regular time and double-time. The objective is to maintain the same constant pulse.

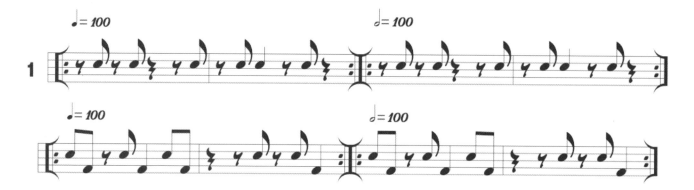

I suggest doing this same kind of thing with all of the coordination exercises discussed in Chapter 1, because there are really only two reasons people lose the groove: they have either a coordination problem which causes the time to fluctuate, or they lose their concentration. So by practicing continually more difficult coordination material, in time, in four-bar phrases, you will strengthen both your concentration and your coordination, and this has to improve your groove.

PLAY-ALONGS

Groove Exercise #2

Another way to improve your groove is to take one tempo, a single tempo, and see how many other tempos you can superimpose over it. So here's an exercise where you start with a slow 4 tempo and then modulate to the quarter-note triplet rate, then modulate to double-time, then to the double-time triplet rate and finally to quadruple the original tempo. So I am thinking of this as being in 4: 1 2 3 4, then thinking of 6 over that: 1 2 3 4 5 6, then going to double time: 1 2 3 4 5 6 7 8, and to 6 over that: 1 2 3 4 5 6 7 8 9 10 11 12, and to double time again: 1 2 3 4 5 6 7 8 9 10 11 12 13 14 15 16. Then, work your way back down to the original tempo.

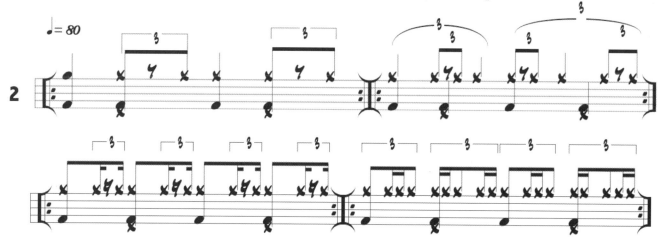

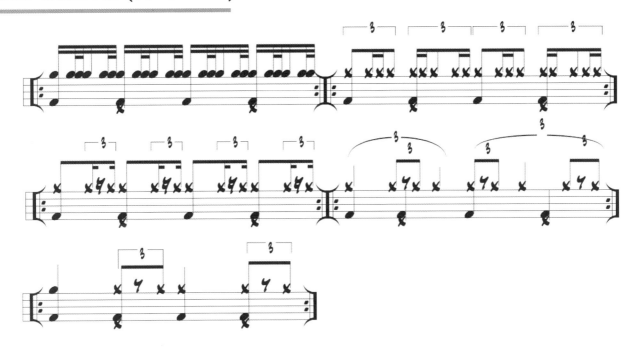

This is a really good exercise to strengthen your time. You can take it a step further by having your feet accelerate along with the cymbal, and that sounds like this:

When playing slow tempos, because there is a lot of real time between each beat, it's important to think of a faster subdivision in order to accurately and consistently place each quarter note—when playing slow, think fast. At fast tempos we are already playing the tiny increments of time, so here the issue is staying relaxed—when playing fast, think slow. Think of the half note or the whole note as the primary pulse.

Musical Transitions

Songs are not one-dimensional; they grow and transform. An area where the groove needs special attention is during transitions from one kind of feel, or orchestration, to another, so that the pulse and flow are not upset. One such transition involves switching from brushes to sticks and from sticks to brushes.

Though we have not spoken about playing brushes (specific brush patterns are not our concern here), the focus is on making a seamless transition.

Niels Christiensen

Pat Metheney, Germany, 1990

To me, the distinguishing color of the sound of the brushes is the sound of the sweeping left brush. The distinguishing color of the sound of sticks is the sound of the stick on the ride cymbal. So, when playing brushes and transitioning to sticks, I maintain that left hand brush as long as possible—I pick up the right stick while the left hand continues with the brush. When going from sticks to brushes I pick up the left brush while continuing until the end of the phrase with the right stick. Practice this transition at a moderate tempo and switch every four measures.

Another common transition point, and possible groove interrupter, occurs when we have to shift from swing to Latin and from Latin to swing. Before we discuss that, I'd like to demonstrate a collection of jazzy Latin grooves. These are not official Afro-Cuban or Brazilian grooves, but really just some things I've seen Max Roach, Philly Joe Jones, Arthur Taylor, Art Blakey, Elvin Jones and others play. I am a huge fan of Latin music and suggest you investigate the masters of that world too.

Notice that, regardless of which rhythm I am playing, the groove remains solid.

Transitioning from one feel to another requires that the drummer be aware of the up-coming shift and that he plays something to help his bandmates and the music turn that corner. When playing swing and going to Latin, a smooth transition requires the drummer to anticipate the upcoming shift and to telegraph it to his bandmates by playing a simple Latin sounding fill in the last measure of the swing section. When going from Latin to swing we do the opposite: in the last measure of the Latin section we play a swing fill to ease the band back into that groove. Let me demonstrate this by playing eight measures of swing into eight measures of Latin.

Conclusion

All of these exercises are designed to help you strengthen your pulse and your awareness of the groove and to help you feel four-measure phrases. So practice the different single-time double-time exercises, practice the accelerating and decelerating through the time exercise, work on your transitions and, at all times, sing the melody to yourself. Practice with a metronome and with recordings of great rhythm sections. Record yourself often to see what the truth is about your groove. Are the problems general—like everything rushes or drags—or specific: certain tempos are difficult to hold, or the time is fluctuating most during fills? This knowledge will guide your practicing.

Groove is really important. Focus on playing in the center of the beat. You want your pulse to be married to the bass player. The goal is to generate a super-stable, buoyant and infectious pulse for your bandmates and the listeners alike. For example, here are a number of choruses of the twelve-bar blues. Each chorus I add a little comping density, but notice that regardless of how simple or complex the comping is, the groove remains solid and infectious.

Groovin' the Blues  PLAY-ALONG

Refer to page 82 for a complete transcription.

Susan Riley

Ron Carter, Manhattan School of Music, 2022

CHAPTER 3: Creativity ▶

So the four components, the four qualities, that are necessary to be a great player are technique, groove, creativity and musicianship. Now I'd like to talk about creativity and use a collection of classic jazz solo phrases as the basis for developing creativity.

Language

The ancient language of Latin is the root of the diverse modern languages of French, Italian, English, Spanish, German and many others. Understanding Latin gives one insight into the vocabulary of each of its descendants. Since everyone playing drums before 1960 was a jazz drummer, the jazz drumming vocabulary is the root of all modern drumming and the basis of this material. As such, this material will be beneficial to anyone interested in playing drums better.

It's said that music, like ancient Latin, is a language and that we learn it the same way we learn any language. So, how did I learn to speak? First I imitated the sounds I heard my parents make without attaching any meaning to them. Soon I realized who "Mommy," "Daddy" and "Johnny" were. Then I learned "yes" and "no" and the meaning of many other sounds. In time I figured out how to organize these sounds to convey what was important to me. Music is learned in a similar fashion. First, we imitate a sound; we learn "ba-da-boom." This is the "what." Then we assimilate; we learn "why" someone played "ba-da-boom." Finally, we begin to innovate by re-ordering the phrases we "know" to express our individual musical vision: "ba-da-ba-da-boom." The difference between learning to speak and music is that in music, you can pick who your parents are!

Monica Cortes

Batuka, Sao Paulo, Brazil, 2010

How do we develop as players? The first thing we need is exposure—we have to be exposed to some music that tickles our ear and makes us curious to know more. It happened for me the first time I saw the Beatles on TV as a youngster. Next, we have to dedicate time to understanding why that music draws us in; what are the specifics? I played along with the radio, and 45-rpm records of my favorite songs, imitating what I thought was being played. Finally, persistent, diligent work led to a kind of flow playing those songs.

After I learned Ringo's language, Gene Krupa's playing, and then the playing of dozens of other musicians tickled my ear in exactly the same way, and I went through the same process of emulation. My teachers and other musicians gave me all kinds of eye-and ear-opening advice and encouragement. Playing in bands allowed me to see just how thoroughly I had assimilated the music. I continue to develop in exactly the same fashion today; I am most dedicated and most focused on developing the things I am most curious about in this moment.

Musical Signals

We've all had the experience of playing a song with a band and having one of the other musicians play a reference to another song. I know when that happens it makes me feel good because it's an indication that that musician and I have enjoyed listening to the same recordings. He plays a quote from one song inside another song, and that sends a signal that influences how I play the music. I may recall the way the song that the quote came from went and have that shape my accompaniment of him because I know he likes that kind of song.

This kind of communication is not a one-way street. It's not just guitar players sending signals to drummers, or saxophone players sending it to drummers. Drummers can send these signals to the other musicians as well. We do this by playing phrases that they might have heard in their favorite recordings. So, like the simple coordination stuff we started with, I'd like to give you a collection of classic jazz phrases that will help you improve your movement around the drums and will give you lots of ideas for creating interesting solos.

Vocabulary

The first phrase is a two-measure phrase that Max Roach often played. It's in sixteenth notes: six notes on the high tom, six notes on the snare, a paradiddle on the floor tom, a paradiddle between the snare and floor tom, then four notes on the snare, four notes on the high tom and four notes on the snare.

What I particularly like about this phrase is the way it changes direction. Max was a master of elegant hand combinations. His movements are most efficient—always moving on the easy hand. He incorporates the paradiddle in the middle of the phrase to help him change direction.

The next phrase is a much simpler one, but it was played by many of the greats. It's an eighth-note phrase broken up between the snare drum and bass drum.

Now if I combine that phrase with the first phrase, you get something like this:

In this example I was thinking in double time: 1234,1234,1234,1234. Let me play it again, thinking regular time.

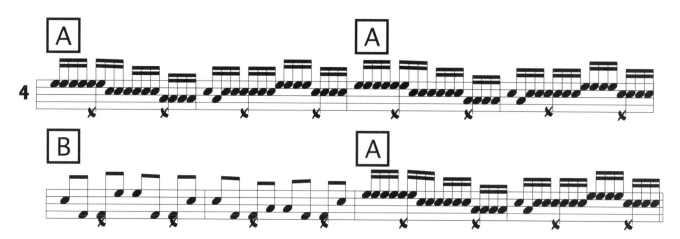

I hope you noticed the way I organized those two phrases. I played the first phrase twice, the Max Roach phrase, then I played the phrase with just the right hand once. I concluded the story by repeating the first phrase again and that tied a nice bow on the entire phrase by giving it a clear symmetry. In fact, many songs have a similar kind of construction where they play a phrase and then they repeat that phrase. Then they play a new phrase and conclude by coming back to the first phrase. This structure is referred to as AABA. The first phrase is called A, and A is repeated. The new phrase is called B, and we conclude with a final repetition of A. This is a very logical structure, and it's really useful to help us communicate our ideas.

The next phrase is based on eighth-note triplets, and it unfolds across the barline by suggesting the idea of playing in 3/4 over 4/4.

That's a phrase that Max Roach played, that Art Blakey played, that Roy Haynes played, that Philly Joe Jones played, and it can be integrated with the first two phrases as well.

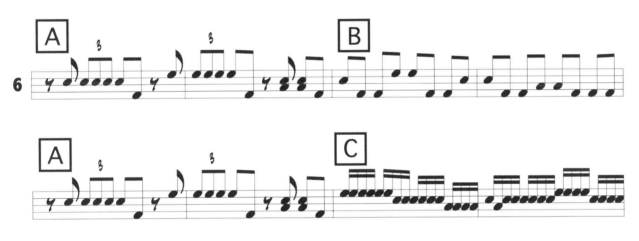

Iowa Day of Percussion, 2010

The rudiments are the ABCs of drumming, but the jazz language gives you information about the correct dialect, the correct way to accent these phrases and the correct way to organize them to tell a story.

The first phrase is based on the five-stroke roll. Jazz drummers often play the five-stroke roll concluding with a stick shot.

In order to get a good sound you have to dig the second left double into the head so that you get a clean sound when the right stick strikes the left. You want a really dry, crisp sound.

When I play it on the high tom you can hear how much pressure I'm putting on the head with my left stick. Listen to how much the pitch bends.

Now we take the five-stroke roll, concluding with a stick shot, and move it around the drums.

The next phrase also employs the stick shot moving the right hand between the snare drum, stick shot, cymbal and floor tom. This is a phrase Philly Joe Jones often played:

Range Recording, Ardmore, PA, 2009

Combined with the other phrases, it sounds like this:

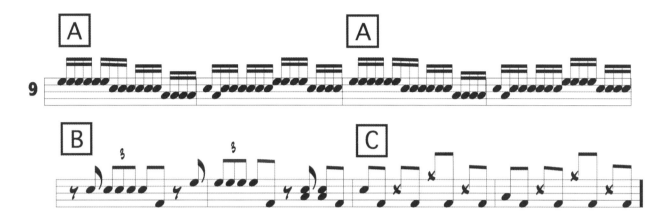

These are all really useful phrases for creating a sense of storytelling.

The next phrase is based on the paradiddle, and we often play the paradiddle with a particular accent pattern. We accent the first right in the right paradiddle and we accent the right inside the left paradiddle so it sounds like this: **R**LRR L**R**LL **R**LRR L**R**LL.

Then that accented note is transposed onto the other drums giving you this kind of sound:

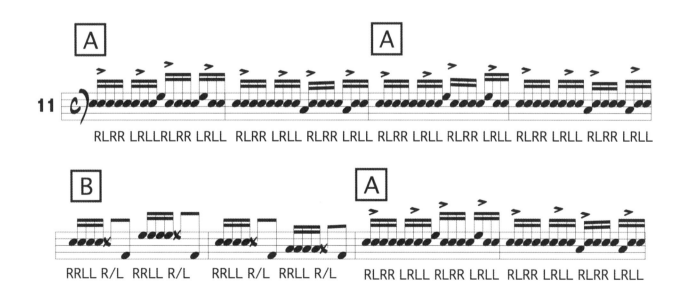

Here's another Max Roach-type phrase. Again, note the elegance in the movement and the nice question-and-answer motif on the toms.

Here's another use of the five-stroke roll. This time it's moving between the floor tom and the snare drum and implying 3/4 over 4/4. I'll play a right five on the floor tom and a left five on the snare drum so it moves back and forth, like this:

So the entire phrase sounds like this:

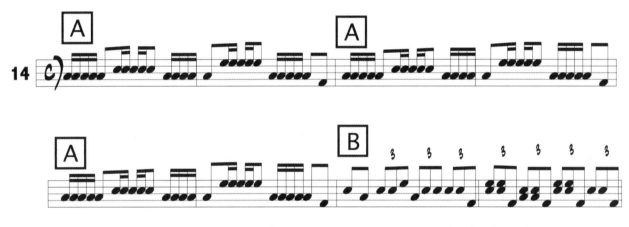

Australia's Ultimate Drummer's Weekend, 2016

Here's a great Roy Haynes-type phrase which embraces the stick shot and implies 3/4.

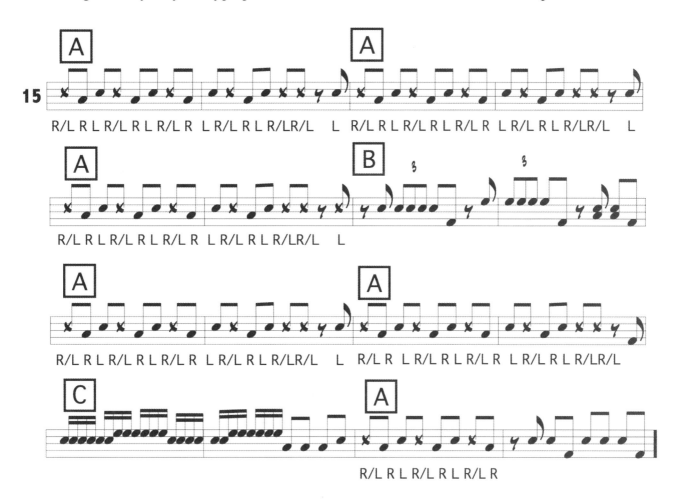

Here's a close cousin to the last phrase, also implying 3/4.

Another three-beat phrase that was often played by the great Philly Joe Jones sounds like this. I'll play it first, then I'll explain the sticking.

These are eighth-note triplets. He's playing the 3/4 ride cymbal pattern in his right hand and accenting the beginning of it each time. The left hand plays the in-between notes.

On the drums it sounds like this:

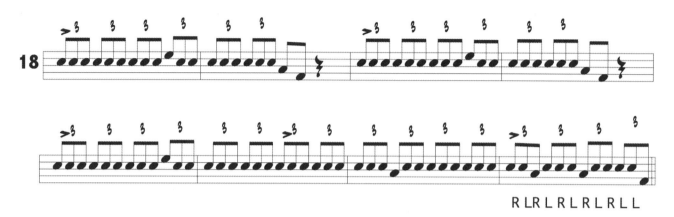

A great phrase using paradiddles but moving them around the kit is playing paradiddles in this fashion:

Here's another great triplet phrase from Max Roach. Notice the elegant movement and how he's always moving to the new drum on the easy hand.

One of the simplest classic jazz phrases is built off of the three-stroke drag. We often play, in Wilcoxon and that kind of snare drum repertoire, mostly right hand drags—LLR, LLR. When playing the kit, the opposite sticking—RRL, RR L—is easier to transpose around the drums. A typical application is this:

Another phrase from Philly Joe Jones employs doubles on the bass drum and singles moving between to floor tom and snare drum, like this:

Finally we have a phrase, again in eighth-note triplets, where the right hand accents on the beat and the left hand accents off the beat.

The unaccented notes are doubles with the opposite hand, so the sticking is:
RLL **R**LL **R**LL RR**L** RR**L** RR**L** **R**LL RR**L**

It should be obvious by now that I love the drums. I wanted to learn all these phrases simply because they tickled my ear the first time I heard them. Transcribing the phrases that tickle your ear is a great way to learn the drumming language. The way you combine and morph that material will evolve into your own voice on the instrument.

"Black Nile" in the Practice Room

Right now I'd like to take a little detour into my practice room at home and show you how I practiced an Elvin Jones solo found in one of my books, *The Jazz Drummer's Workshop*. First I learned the individual elements; here I've pieced the solo together starting at 130 beats per minute and very gradually work it up to the original tempo. It's important not to tense up or alter the solo as you increase the tempo.

Germany, 1988

Conclusion

So now what do you do with all this material? Practice the individual phrases to get a flow with each of them. Once you are comfortable, make a structured scheme to connect each of the phrases together—practice the first phrase into the second one, the first one into the third one, the first one into the fourth one, etc. Then play the second phrase into the first one, the second phrase into the third one, the second phrase into the fourth one and so on until you're comfortable weaving all the possible combinations from the collection seamlessly together.

Work with different phrase structure, for example **AABA**, **AABC**, **ABCA**, **ABBC**, etc. Remember, whichever phrase you play first, that's **A**. Whichever phrase is introduced second, that's **B**. The third phrase is **C**. Next, add rests to the phrases. Vary your dynamics. Add ideas inspired by the playing of your idols—transcribing IS a great tool—and ideas of your own invention. This material isn't necessarily intended to replace everything you currently play, it's simply intended to inform and fortify the content of your playing. You'll be amazed at how many combinations are possible and how practicing in this fashion improves your flow and musicality at the kit.

Finally, deconstruct the phrases by cutting and pasting them; in other words, take a phrase and loop it back on itself before its natural conclusion. For example, if we take the very first phrase, the two-measure Max Roach sixteenth-note idea, and play the first measure and the first beat of the second measure, then jump back to the beginning again, we come up with a really nice, modern sounding five-beat loop like this:

Max Five-Beat Loop

RLRR LRLL   RLRR LRLL   RLRR LRLL

By varying your dynamics, adding rests, changing the rate to double-time or half-time, and cutting and pasting these ideas you can come up with a vast array of great phrases. So your goal with the material is not to become a clone, but rather to really learn how to hear good drumming "words" and then to freely use and embellish them to convey your own perspective on the music.

Along those lines: The first time subbed for Mel Lewis at the Village Vanguard, I was called in at the last minute because Mel had a family emergency. In those days the band played three sets starting at 10 p.m. I got the call at 9:50 and ran down to the club. They had already begun, and saxophonist Joe Lovano had moved from his regular chair back to Mel's drums to play the first tune. I finished that set and the next one. By the end of the second set Mel had arrived in the club. I went over to him and asked him if he was going to play the third set. He said: "No, I like what you're doing." Then he added: "I can tell you love this music. Play it the way YOU hear it."

CHAPTER 4: Musicianship ▶

Lessons Learned on the Bandstand

We've discussed technique, we've discussed groove and we've discussed creativity. Musicianship is really the assimilation of all those components and the integration of them with a band. So, in addition to having good time and fluid movement, making good judgments about what to play is the final piece of the puzzle.

As a student at North Texas, I was really stimulated by my teachers and the other students. The only down side of being there was that Denton, Texas wasn't a stop on the touring schedule of many bands in those days. I can count on one hand the number of times I got to hear one of the legends play live. There was a club in Dallas called Mother Blues which occasionally booked jazz acts, and I was excited to learn that Dizzy Gillespie was set to do a couple nights there. To be honest, at age 19 I didn't really know much about Dizzy except that he was a jazz icon, so I should go hear him. The music I was most captivated with at that time was the music of John Coltrane with Elvin Jones, Miles Davis with Tony Williams and the contemporary bands like Tower of Power and Weather Report. Bebop wasn't really on my radar screen yet.

Anyway, I made a reservation to see Dizzy on his second night at Mother Blues. Some of my schoolmates went the first night and returned to tell me how great the concert was and that they especially loved Dizzy's drummer Mickey Roker. This made me anticipate the concert even more.

So I went to the club and when I checked in the doorman said, "You're John Riley? We've been trying to reach you because we heard you are a good jazz drummer. Mickey Roker got suddenly ill and can't play tonight, so you've got to play with Dizzy." As I said, I didn't know Dizzy's music and nearly died on the spot.

Well, I met Dizzy on the bandstand and he was really relaxed and kind of joking around; this was comforting. Before the first tune he announced to the audience that they were in for a very special evening because he was introducing a new talent that he just discovered—and I hadn't played a note!

Dizzy turned his back to the audience and said to me: "We're going to start with 'Con Alma.' Do you know it?" I said, "No." He said, "No problem. It's in 12/8, whatever that means to you." We played "Con Alma"; I have no idea what it sounded like, but it felt really easy to me. Afterwards, Dizzy turned to me and said, "We're going to play 'Salt Peanuts.' Do you know it?" I said, "Sorry, no." He said, "That's OK. It is a fast swinger. You start it, whatever tempo you like." The rest of the night proceeded in the same fashion. I'm certain I didn't sound anything like Mickey Roker, but Dizzy was really encouraging. After the gig he gave me his number and told me to look him up if I ever get to New York.

So what's the point of my telling this story? My point is that the truly great musicians understand how, and make adjustments, to play together. Dizzy knew that it would be easier for him to hear just what I was capable of and adjust his playing to that reality than it would be for me—the young, inexperienced, aspiring post-bop drummer—to adjust. Dizzy could have made me look like a fool on the bandstand by playing things that I couldn't deal with, but he knew that that would be no great accomplishment for him, that it would not make pleasant listening for the audience and that it would depress me to no end.

The lesson from Dizzy is this: Musicianship means seeing the big picture and doing everything you are capable of to make the music as a whole sound as good as possible.

As my experience with Dizzy showed us, it's really helpful to have an appreciation and understanding of the challenges the other musicians are going through when they are playing. That information will inform you how to accompany them.

With Dizzy Gillespie at Mother Blues, Dallas, Texas, 1974

Musical Structure

Our bandmates are dealing with the melody, so it's crucial that we know the melody to the songs we are playing. One way to get more familiar with a song is to learn its lyrics. Knowing the lyrics will help you retain the melody more easily, and it will also give you an idea about the mood of the song, and that should help your interpretation too. You can learn the lyrics to many songs by listening to the recordings of Frank Sinatra, Ella Fitzgerald and Sarah Vaughan.

Our bandmates are playing over the harmonic cycle or form of the song, so it's crucial that we can hear that structure. The two most common forms or structures that we deal with are the AABA form that I mentioned earlier—it's often a 32-measure form of 8+8+8+8—and the twelve-bar blues. You need to be able to hear those structures unfolding and repeating without resorting to counting the measures.

Among the play-along tracks included with this package is a 32-measure AABA tune we refer to as "rhythm changes," which is based on the harmonic cycle of George Gershwin's "I've Got Rhythm." This harmonic cycle is the basis for many jazz and popular songs. One popular rhythm changes tune is the theme from "The Flintstones" cartoon show. If you can sing that song to yourself, it will help you feel the AABA structure. It would be a good idea to get even more familiar with this by spending some time working your way through this chord sequence at the piano or on a guitar.

Another of the play-along tracks is a twelve-bar blues. Many rock 'n' roll songs are based on the twelve-bar blues, and so is the theme song from the "Batman" cartoon show. Use that melody as a reference point as you practice the drums, and get comfortable playing the blues on the harmonic instrument of your choice.

Control Room Analysis

Now I'd like to listen to a recording that I did with a quartet and discuss how I am integrating all these ideas, in the groove, and how the communication between the band members dictates what I play. The idea is to use our ears to direct our limbs to create a sympathetic accompaniment and to keep the music growing.

When we're trading solos, we want our ideas to relate and connect to each other so that there is a continuous melodic line running through the music. One musician will play some kind of motivic material, and I'm listening for a tiny fragment that I can transfer to the drums, make a drum version of, and then boomerang back. It's not simply a matter of playing the licks that we've been talking about; it's a matter of integrating them in a logical fashion within the context of the music in that moment. So let's go into the control room and listen to this track.

We're here in the control room at Range Studio with Brian R., and I'd like to tie all the themes we've been discussing thus far together by listening to a live recording I made number of years ago with a quartet consisting of George Garzone on saxophone, Kenny Werner on piano and Ed Schuller on bass.

Nick Meyer

Range Recording, Ardmore, PA, 2009

What I'd like to do is listen to the trading section of the song and stop after each of the piano or saxophone trades and discuss what I heard in their playing and then listen to how I reacted to what they did, because the idea of a theme continuing through the song is really important—it's a conversation among the musicians.

This particular song is a twelve-measure structure. It's not a blues, but it's a twelve-measure structure, and at this point we've been playing for seven or eight minutes and the bass solo is just concluding. He has sent a signal to us that he is wrapping up his solo by making a reference to the melody. That's often the way people conclude their solos. They either get much softer in volume or they'll play a reference to the melody and that's an indication that their improvising is done. The other musicians at that point have the option of returning to the melody, and ending the song, or having a drum solo or having some kind of trading. In this case we trade twelve-measure choruses. The piano plays the first chorus. Let's listen to what Kenny played and see how I reacted to it.

What I heard Kenny play was a motivic idea based on a 5/8 rhythm. I took that structure and made a drum version of it, trying to tie these two sections together. In the end I distorted it and threw it back to George Garzone. So listen to Kenny's solo and see if you can hear the 5/8 motif that he plays and how I develop it on the drums.

Can you hear the 5/8 motif? Now, it's difficult to feel that kind of asymmetrical phrase going through the time. You have several kinds of accounting going on in your mind: You've got to maintain the integrity of the phrase, but more importantly you've got to keep your place in 4/4 and feel the whole twelve measures regardless of how asymmetrical your improvisation is.

Let's listen again to see if your can hear that little motif, how I picked up on it, and how George picks up with what I did.

George doesn't really take the idea that Kenny and I are developing, but what I hear is that at the conclusion of his twelve-measure phrase is this melodic idea that sounds like he's going out of time. I got the impression that he was trying to sound like he was drunk. It gets really wobbly in the time, and when I start my drum solo I'm trying to capture that mood and carry it into the next section the song. Let's listen to George's twelve and my twelve to see if you can hear that connection. Listen particularly to the very end of his phrase and how it feels off-kilter, and hear the way I'm capturing that same feeling.

Now Kenny generates an incredible amount of momentum in his twelve-measure phrase. After what he played, I had the feeling that I couldn't compete with the intensity he generated. At the beginning of my next exchange, I leave some silence to let that tension dissipate a little bit, so I can get a fresh start at a level that I can build from into the next phrase. We'll listen to what Kenny played and how the energy increases and increases, giving me nowhere to go, so I kind of let the balloon burst for a second and then resume. We'll listen to Kenny, my trade and then see what George does after that.

So George kind of takes the material that I'm developing at the end of my solo and begins his twelve-measure phrase with something that resembles what I left him with. Now, at the end of his solo he plays a motivic idea that I grab for my next twelve—he plays an idea that's based on the rhythm +2 +4 +2 +4, and I try to make a drum version of that and then boomerang the whole thing back to Kenny for his next exchange.

Let's hear where George started, listen for the +2 +4 motif where it sounds like the time is turned around, and see if you can hear the drum version of that little idea.

I think it was pretty vivid the way that the motivic material got tossed from one player to another. During Kenny's next exchange, he plays a run of eighth notes, and I can't really find a structure that I'm going to grab, so I play some running eighth notes to create a melody that's somehow complementary, even if it isn't literally related to what he plays.

Here's Kenny's phrase and my phrase again, and we'll continue on the next one.

George leaves me with a very nice motivic idea to develop: +2 +3 +4 +. I find a way to make a drum phrase out of that.

Let's check it out again: how he ends his solo and how I build my twelve measures off of his motivic idea.

CHAPTER 4 (continued)

Kenny takes the energy that I'm playing with and really reaches a high peak in his solo. We've been talking about technique all day—technique of the hands, technique of coordination, technique of integrating phrases together. The part of technique that is really critical for a high level of musicianship is not simply having fast hands or having amazing coordination. It's having fast ears so you can react to what's going on around you, so you can make the judgments that the other musicians make seem like brilliant choices. That's our job as accompanists: to make whatever the other guys are doing seem like it's absolutely the right thing. One is fortunate if you have the opportunity to play with like-minded musicians who make your choices sound like the right choices. This kind of internal communication keeps the music fresh. If we simply play the licks that we know, then it's a forgone conclusion what's going to happen. If there's an organic, rolling nature to the music then it's more fun to play, more interesting to listen to, and there's a possibility for something really creative to happen.

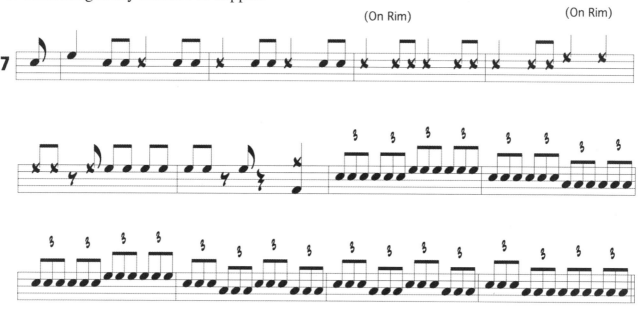

Australia's Ultimate Drummer's Weekend, 2016

I hope you heard the connection between the fast, dark-sounding fill I played at the end of my phrase and the way George picked up his solo in the same kind of mood. At the end of George's phrase, he begins to bring the dynamics down, and that's a suggestion that maybe we are going to wrap up the trading section. I play one more twelve-measure section and kind of imply the melody. I thin out the density and the volume of what I'm playing and play shapes that are similar to the melody. This sends a clear signal to the other guys that we're going home.

One more time, from George's solo into my last twelve-measure solo.

Conclusion

I hope that this discussion gives you some insight into the way you can use the material you have, the phrases we've been talking about, and the way you need to integrate them with the people you are playing with. If this ensemble played with a more bebop concept I would be playing different vocabulary. The vocabulary is always dictated by the mood, expressiveness, and types of content that the other musicians are playing. That's what musicianship is all about. It's about connecting everything that everyone plays to make the sum of the parts greater than the individual parts. Musicians that play this was always have opportunities to work because their playing embraces the choices that the others make and the music remains fresh. I hope you've gained some insight from this discussion.

TRANSCRIPTIONS

Thanks for your interest in this supplemental material to my DVD, *The Master Drummer*. I was inspired to write this book by requests from many drummers who have enjoyed watching the DVD and asked for more, and by Terry Branam, who has done incredibly accurate transcriptions of my playing from the parts of *The Master Drummer* that were not included in the ebook that is part of the original DVD .

The process of putting together the DVD was fun and a lot of work. When I was preparing to film, my focus was on the content and the best way to organize and present the material. At the end of our day shooting, my videographer Tony Scimeca, whose focus was on capturing the material and making sure we had everything needed for the complete DVD, said, "You know, we need some footage to use under the menu page and credits, we need some flash." Well, I hadn't really thought about our needs in those areas, and I certainly hadn't prepared any flashy solo material, but I knew we had to get all the filming we needed right at that moment, so I played three brief solos which are the solos you see during the menu page, behind the final credits and in the bonus footage as "Solo 3." Terry's transcriptions of those solos and the "In the Woodshed" segment make up the bulk of the music in this section. I've added detailed commentary about the construction, phrases and inspiration behind these segments.

Studying the material in this book will give you insight into the playing process "in the moment," it will add to your understanding of additional ideas one might play, the reasons behind them and much more. Enjoy!

55 Bar with Harvie S., 1992

Alessandro Della Valle

All my public playing is done with other people; I have never done a solo concert. I find the give and take of playing with great players inspiring and prefer to play in an organic, in-the-moment fashion. Ideas, musical "food," from the others always propels me to explore new ideas. The discovery and exploration of new material with great players is one of the most compelling reasons I play. Obviously, when filming the DVD, I was playing alone and couldn't draw on the ideas of bandmates.

Sometimes, fortunately very rarely these days, I will be on a gig but will not find myself particularly well "fed" or inspired by the ideas from the others. On those rare occasions I have few options; I can play based on the lack of input and therefore sound uninspired, or I can play something I "know" and use that as a launching point to improvise from. That's the approach taken in these short solo pieces.

OPENING SOLO

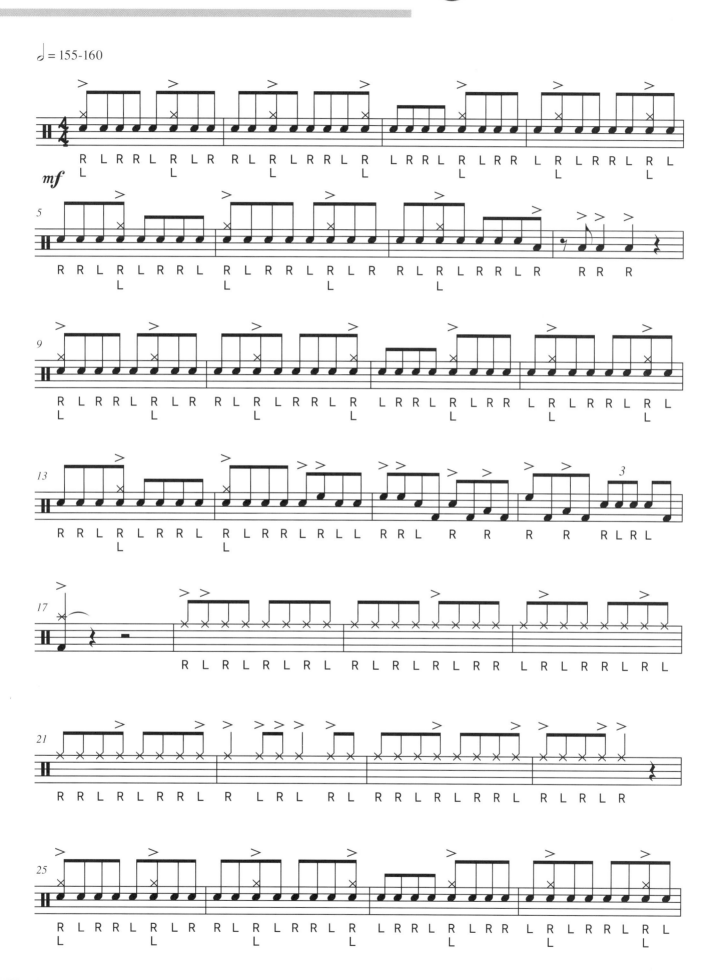

John Riley – The Master Drummer

OPENING SOLO Breakdown

The Opening Solo begins with a 5/8 phrase that I've practiced and like. It's flam left 5-stroke rolls played consecutively, without any gap between them. The flammed 5s are played for the bulk of the first two eight-measure phrases, bars 1-8 and 9-16, and they unfold across many barlines. Although many drummers have explored playing 5/8 phrases in 4/4, the first example I can think of is Max Roach's groove, recorded in 1951, on Bud Powell's song "Un Poco Loco." I play a version of Max's groove later on the DVD: it's the sixth Latin rhythm with the cowbell. Flammed 5s like this were first employed by Tony Williams in the 1960s, and have become quite common since the 1990s. Here's my sticking pattern and a couple other sticking patterns for 5-note phrases:

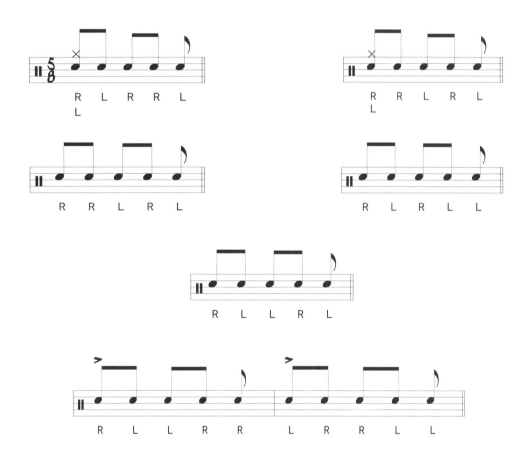

Please notice how in measure 8 I break the 5-note pattern to resolve the phrase, and in measures 15 and 16 the pattern I break it to transition and move the solo forward.

Measures 17-24 contrast bars 1-16 by moving off the drums and onto the hi-hat, but you can see a 5/8 idea still helps form the phrase from beat 3 of bar 19 through bar 23.

In measure 25, the flam 5s return and run through bar 31; bar 32 is a transitional measure into the next section of the solo.

The first 32 measures of the solo are structured like the most common song form: AABA. Measures 1-8, 9-16 and 25-32 explore one "theme" (flam 5s) while the B section, measures 17-25, are a related theme but in a different key—the key of the hi-hat.

In measure 33 a new theme appears and begins a long series of four-bar question-and-answer type phrases—more or less equivalent to the "solo" after the stating of the "melody" in the first 32 bars. This new motif is a relative of the flammed 5s played earlier: flammed 7s. The first question—the 7s—runs from 33-34 and 41-42. Bars 37-40 and 45-48 answer.

Here's the flam 7 phrase and a couple other ways to stick and orchestrate it:

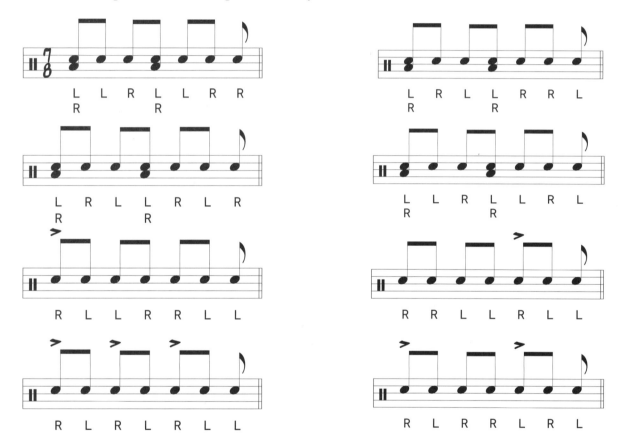

Measures 35-36 and 44 consist of hand and foot combinations. Here are some building blocks for this kind of material:

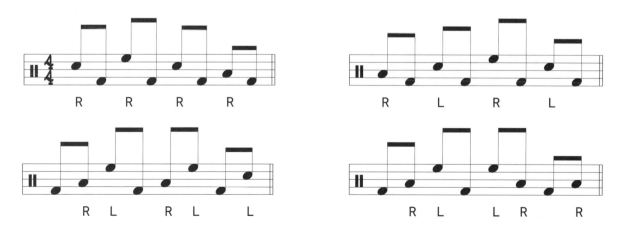

Measures 45-48 feature single-stroke 8th-note triplets around the drums. This phrase will really help you to develop these kinds of ideas:

R L R L R L R L R L R L

Measures 49-64 explore another 7-note phrase based on the 6-stroke roll plus one note with the foot and a 3-note RL foot combination. Get comfortable with these motifs:

R L L R R L   R L L R R L

Measure 65 is a Tony Williams drag idea. 66-68 is more triplets around the drums. Here's the drag idea and a variation:

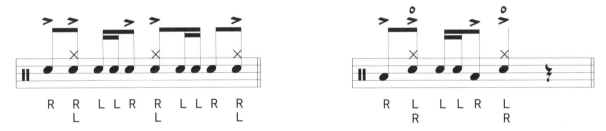

R R L L R R L L R R   R L L L R L
L   L   L   R   R

Measures 69-76 include a little cousin of the 7-note idea first played in bar 50. You might call it a paradiddle-diddle with the hi-hat substituting for the last left hand:

R L R R L   R L   R R L   R L R

Philly Joe Jones was a great exponent of the kind of hand and foot combinations played in bars 77-80. Here is one of his motifs:

R   R   R/L   R   R   R/L   R L R L

Measures 81-88 and 89-96 shift gears and move on to the ride cymbal while developing broken three-beat Latin phrases between the toms and the feet. This is the building block for developing similar ideas:

Measure 97 returns to the original flam 5 motif and signals the beginning of the end of the solo. Revisiting the original theme is a common device used in classical music and is referred to as the "recapitulation."

The final 16 bars of this solo feature snippets of many of the main motifs introduced previously. Closing a solo in this fashion sends a clear signal to your audience that you are concluding your musical story.

As I mentioned earlier, I had not given any forethought to playing this solo or any of the other solos but I simply used the resources at hand: motivic material I had developed and liked, an awareness of phrase symmetry and pacing, and finally, the desire to tell some kind of story in the solo. Developing the main motifs presented here, then personalizing them, will go a long way in helping you play in a flowing and musically mature fashion.

Woody Herman, Arizona, 1978

CLOSING SOLO

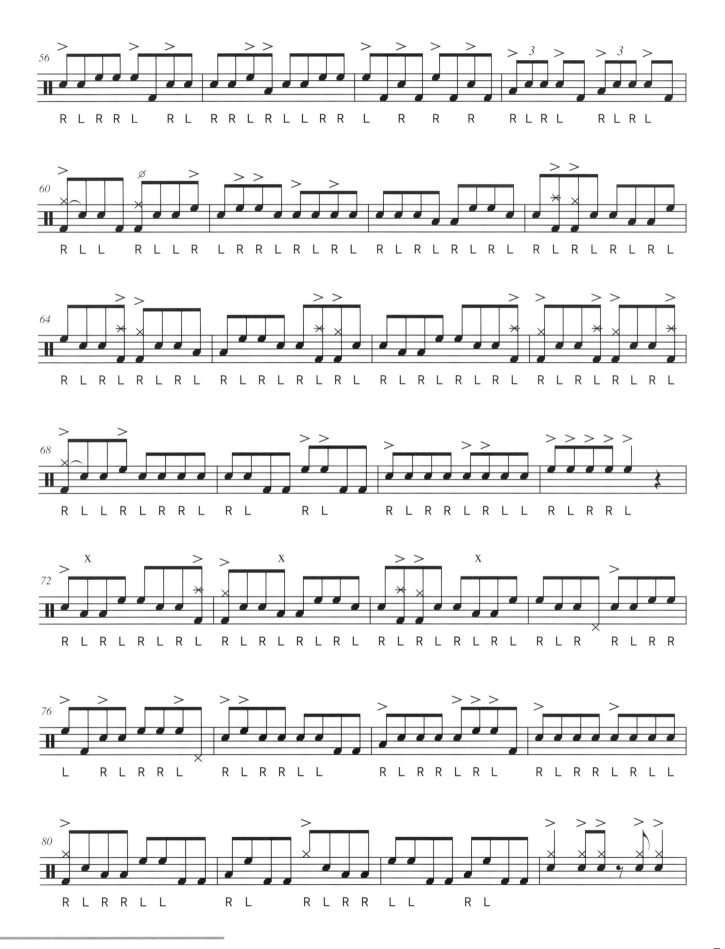

John Scofield and Joe Lovano, England, 1990

CLOSING SOLO Breakdown

When I finished the first solo, I wasn't feeling satisfied, so I immediately played another solo, which became the footage that runs under the closing credits. After the opening seven-measure phrase, the body of this solo is clearly structured in eight-bar phrases and employs similar developmental devices, connective material, paradiddle variations and question-and-answer phrasing to the Opening Solo. As such, there is no need to dig into it in the same detail as the previous solo, but I would like to point out the prime, new motivic ideas dealt with here and encourage you to get comfortable with them too.

The solo opens with a motif reminiscent of some of the ideas Tony Williams played in the 1960s with Miles Davis. The orchestration of this twelve-note phrase, based on the paradiddle-diddle sticking, creates a pleasing melodic shape. Here's the original motif and a couple variations:

Measures 32-35 introduce ideas like those Roy Haynes has used beautifully for decades. Get comfortable with combinations like this:

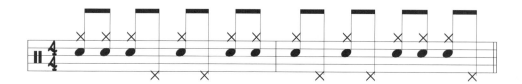

Measure 44 gives a glimpse of a paradiddle phrase that really facilitates smooth, fast movement around the kit:

Measures 62-74 explore a ten-note crossing phrase and its variations. Alex Sanguinetti showed me this idea many years ago. Here's the basic idea:

The opening theme is restated from bar 80 to 95 to signal the close of the solo and to put on a nice bookend.

Nick Meyer

Range Recording, Ardmore, PA, 2009

SOLO 3 ▶

♩ = 145-150

SOLO 3 Breakdown

As I completed the Closing Solo, I was still not content and went right into another attempt. Yes, many components are reminiscent of the previous solos so I will focus on the unique elements.

Solo 3 begins with a roll on the floor tom. Obviously I was thinking of the way many TV award shows open with a timpani roll: "And now, live from..."

In measure 25 a seven-note motif based on a left paradiddle appears. Here's the original and some variations:

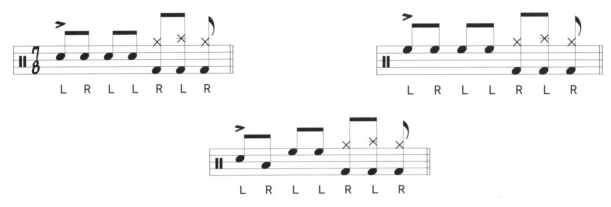

Measures 36 and 43-44 explore triplets grouped in 4s:

Measures 49-59 explore denser versions of material from the opening solo.

Measure 60 introduces singles between the hands and foot which morphs into a three-beat, eighth-note triplet idea in bars 61-63.

The floor tom roll beginning in bar 77 signals the beginning of the end of the solo. The little coda is a typical "signing off" or "closing the door" phrase indicating that "that's all, folks."

IN THE WOODSHED

A couple months before we shot the DVD I bought a video camera to use in my preparations for the filming. The first day I got the camera, I set it up in my practice room to see how well it worked. The "Woodshed" segment is the first few minutes from that afternoon practice session. Months later, as the DVD was being edited, I realized that including a portion of that practice session could be a valuable segment to reinforce a number of themes. In fact, in this segment you can see me practicing many of the ideas discussed and which I played in the three solos described above. Another interesting aspect of this segment is that it really gives a "behind the scenes" perspective to my practice methods.

Every day, before I go to the drums, I warm up on a practice pad. My objective in my 15-minute or so warm-up (see "The Warm-up" in *The Jazz Drummer's Workshop*) is to remind my hands of the feeling of the rebounding sticks, to allow my muscles to relax and align for drumming, and to ponder what I hope to accomplish when I sit down at my kit. My purpose on this particular day was simply to test the audio and video capacities of my new Sony HC1 HD camera while having some fun and refining some ideas at the kit. The result was a fairly free-formed blowing session, structurally much looser than the three solos that I would eventually play and include in this book. As I review it now, some of the material is very familiar to me, and should by now be familiar to you, while other sections sound completely fresh, in the moment, and I have no recollection of ever working on or playing these ideas. Ah, "new" material to explore!

Jimmy Katz/Giant Steps

Visiones Jazz Club, NYC, 1985

IN THE WOODSHED

♩ = 126

mf

RRLLRL

RLRRLLRR LLRLLLRRL RLRLRRL

RLRLRLRLL RRLRLLLRLRLRL RLRLRLRLRLRL

John Riley – The Master Drummer

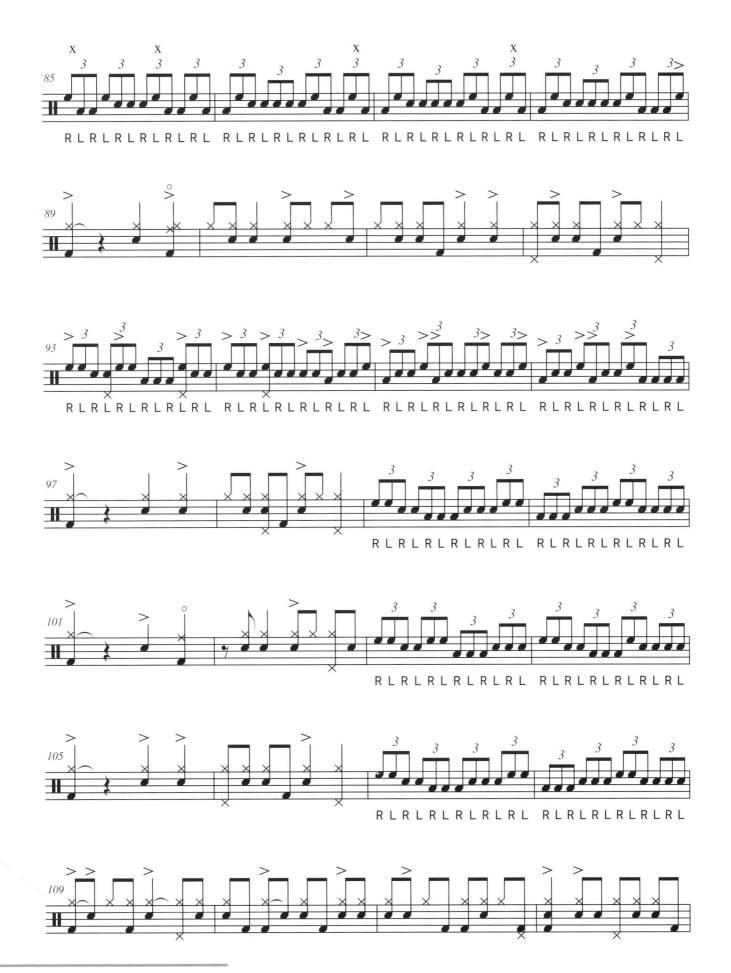

John Riley – The Master Drummer

IN THE WOODSHED Breakdown

Since this wasn't a solo per se, and many of the individual ideas played here have already been discussed, a complete analysis is not necessary. What I would like to bring to your attention is that, in addition to the coordination material and references to all the Max, Roy, Philly Joe and Elvin ideas we've discussed, the time playing from the beginning through measure 149 of this segment is broken up between the four limbs in a way that is certainly inspired and informed by the playing of Tony Williams and Jack DeJohnette. From measure 258 on, the time playing is definitely inspired by Elvin Jones.

Some of the material I played here did not appear in the official solos, but is worth another look. In terms of how to best approach this material: I suggest listening to it and following Terry's clear transcription. Feel free to stop and examine any little bit or longer phrase you are drawn to, take those ideas to your kit to explore, get comfortable with, personalize and integrate with your vocabulary. That's exactly the way I do it when exposed to new material.

Susan Riley

Cornwall on Hudson, NY, 2009

Measures 33-40 explore three and four-note Swiss mill combinations and generate another type of seven-note motif. Here's the original sticking and a couple orchestrations:

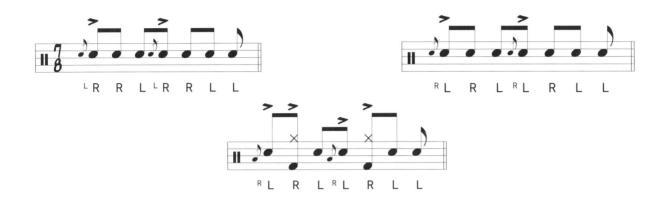

The crossing patterns in bars 85-88 and 93-97 create nice melodies and begin a long practice segment exploring Max-like triplet ideas around the drums. The basic ideas are these:

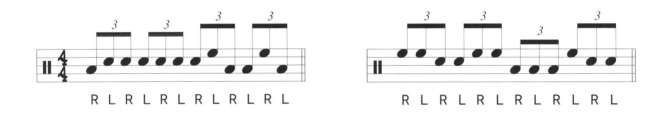

Measures 99-100 are precisely the Max phrase played in Chapter 3.

Measures 125-149 I am coasting and pondering what to explore next.

RHYTHM CHANGES

The term "rhythm changes" refers to the harmonic structure of George Gershwin's song "I've Got Rhythm." Jazz musicians find this specific 32-measure AABA cycle particularly enjoyable to solo over. They have written dozens of new melodies over this cycle and recorded hundreds of versions of rhythm changes, so drummers need to be aware of and comfortable hearing and playing this harmonic cycle. To that end, I have provided eight choruses of this cycle, played by the great bassist Jay Anderson, to play along with. Listening to me play along and following Terry's transcription will give you ideas about some different approaches. Granted, playing duo with bass does invite one to play busier than one might when playing in a larger ensemble, but keeping your place in the AABA cycle and maintaining a good flow for eight choruses at this brisk tempo is great practice. I did not practice playing along with this track before we shot this scene, so what your are hearing is me playing with it for the first time and reacting to the variations in Jay's bass lines, not some prescribed drum part. Enjoy!

Niels Christiensen

John Scofield, Joe Lovano and Anthony Cox, Germany, 1990

RHYTHM CHANGES  PLAY-ALONG

A

John Riley – The Master Drummer

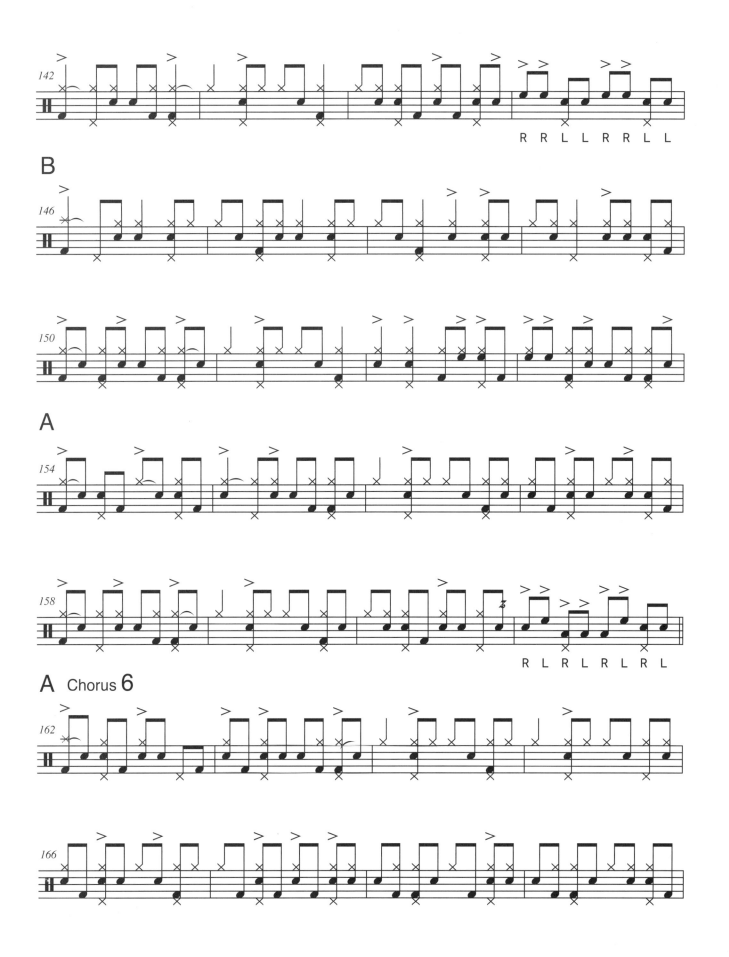

A

B

A

A Chorus 7

A Chorus 8

GROOVIN' THE BLUES

A medium-tempo blues is something every drummer should be comfortable playing. Here Jay Anderson plays eight choruses and I add a little something to my comping in each chorus to propel it forward. The first chorus is simply time on the ride cymbal, feathering the bass drum and two and four on the hi-hat. In the second chorus I add the cross-stick on beat four. For the third chorus, the cross-stick grows into the "bongo beat." The fourth chorus is a common Art Blakey-type comping riff. In the fifth chorus I begin to comp more freely, and choruses six through eight become gradually more dense — but never at the expense of the swinging groove. My approach is intentionally deliberate here, so that something new is happening each chorus to help this simple, basic groove, feel alive and compelling. Try to cultivate order and responsibility in your playing while still giving the music the "lift" it requires.

Jules Follett

PASIC, San Antonio, Texas, 2015

GROOVIN' THE BLUES

♩ = 130   *Swing 8th notes*

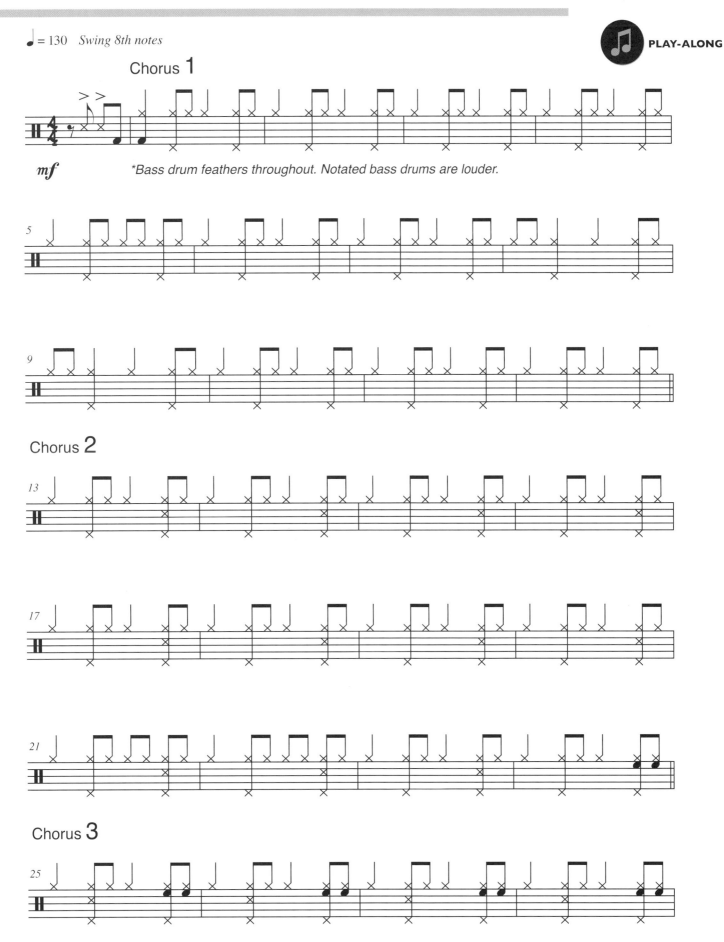

Chorus 4

Chorus 5

Chorus 6

Chorus 7

Chorus 8

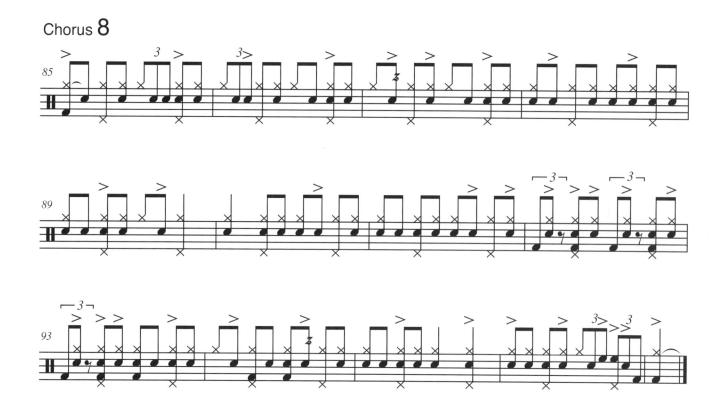

CLOSING STATEMENT

We can't predict the sound of music in the future, but we know it will be created by adventurous and innovative musicians. I am certain that the drummers leading the way will be exceptional musicians with solid technique, a strong groove and a fertile imagination, so the concepts we've been discussing will always be pertinent.

John Riley

ACKNOWLEDGMENTS

John proudly plays Yamaha drums; Zildjian cymbals, sticks and brushes; Remo drumheads and LP percussion.